A SELECTION OF EXISTENTIAL POETRY

Soul's Echoes

Fernando M.S. Silva

FERNANDO M. S. SILVA

Soul's Echoes

Colecção Ecos Lusíadas
Ecos Lusíadas Publications
San Rafael, California, U. S. A.

Wasteland Press
Shelbyville, KY USA
www.wastelandpress.net

Soul's Echoes
by Fernando M.S. Silva

Copyright © 2005 Fernando M.S. Silva
ALL RIGHTS RESERVED

First Printing – December 2005
ISBN: 1-933265-91-4

Printed in the U.S.A.

Other Publications by the Author

The Philosophic and Educational Thought of Antero de Quental
(Doctoral Dissertation) (1968)
University of California, Berkeley, California, U. S. A.

Antero de Quental, The Existentialist Poet-Philosopher,
His Philosophy and Educational Thought (1970)
Atélier Gráfico Novotipo, Lisboa, Portugal

Conselho das Comunidades Portuguesas—1981,
Os Órgãos Luso-Americanos de Comunicação Social (1981)
Secretaria de Estado das Comunidades Portuguesas, Lisboa, Portugal

Antero de Quental, Evolução da sua Filosofia Existencialista
e do seu Pensamento Pedagógico (1986)
Secretaria Regional dos Assuntos Sociais, Açores, Portugal

Perspectivas Histórico-Sociológicas das Comunidades Luso-Californianas
(1986)
II Congresso de Comunidades Açorianas, Terceira, Açores, Portugal

Mais de Um Século de Imprensa Portuguesa na Califórnia (1995)
III Congresso de Comunidades Açorianas, Faial, Açores, Portugal

Ecos Lusíadas no Oeste Americano (1996)
Colecção Ecos Lusíadas, San Rafael, California, U. S. A.

Ecos Lusiadas no Novo Mundo (1997)
Colecção Ecos Lusíadas, San Rafael, California, U. S .A.

Pedaços de Alma --- (Poetry)--- (1996) (1997) (1998)
Colecção Ecos Lusíadas, San Rafael, California, U. S .A.

John Dewey and Karl Jaspers, Main Philosophic Concepts
and Educational Implications (1998)
Colecção Ecos Lusíadas, San Rafael, California, U. S. A.

Notes and Essays on Philosophy, Education & Psychology (1999)
Colecção Ecos Lusíadas, San Rafael, California, -U. S. A.

Os Órgãos Luso-Californianos de Informação e Cultura (1999)
Colecção Ecos Lusíadas, San Rafael, California, U. S. A.

Pedaços de Alma--- Soul's Fragments ---(Poetry)--- (2001)
Colecção Ecos Lusíadas, San Rafael, California, U. S. A.

Perspectivas --- Selecção de Obras em Prosa do Autor --- (2005)
Colecção Décima Ilha
Portuguese Heritage Publications of California, Inc., San José, California, U. S. A.

Anthologies containing selections of the author's poetic works
in English and Portuguese:

Cornucopia—An Anthology of Contemporary Poetry --- (1978)
Contemporary Literature Press -- San Francisco, California, U. S. A.

Antologia Poética dos Açores (1979)
        Compiled and edited by Prof. Dr. Rui Galvão de Carvalho
    Secretaria Regional da Educação e Cultura,
    Angra do Heroísmo, Açores, Portugal

**** The author has published nearly 300 essays, conferences, articles,
    poems, etc. in various publications in the U. S. A. and in Europe.

TABLE OF CONTENTS

PRELIMINARY WORDS

Since the early dawn of humanity, perhaps when the sun first kissed our ancestors with its welcoming sunshine, or when the first falling leaves of autumn were announcing white snows and the gelid winds of winter, or when spring commenced its florid dances and the earth opened up the bounty of Mother Nature, or, undoubtedly, when the first man and the first woman first embraced fervidly in a confirmation of their love, poetry has never ceased to be what it really is: the echo of the human soul.

This echo, multifarious in its modes of interpretation and expression, can be, very often, truly overpowering and sublime, as it penetrates and envelops the hearts and the minds of human beings who, perchance, partake in the perceptions and in the experiences of the poet. Such is the charm and the fascination of authentic poetry that, throughout the centuries, many have asserted frequently that it often surpasses other artistic expressions in the characterization and definition of the innermost aspects of humanity.

The poems selected for this poetic compilation emanate, indeed, from the depths of a soul interlaced with its heart. The verses of SOUL'S ECHOES, conceived in free style, and written mostly in

English, but with a few in Classical Latin, reflect a wide gamut of emotions, which may offer a glimpse into the humanity of the poet. With utmost care and feeling, he depicts and interweaves a variety of existential perceptions, interpretations and interplays, ranging from meta-physical as well as philosophical preoccupations to concerns relating to other spheres of human interaction. These elements are so dominant in his thoughts that, at times, they even pervade his various amatory verses, either those that may be of phantasmagoric nature, or the ones that are perceived as undeniably real.

SOUL'S ECHOES is, of course, a synoptic account of an existential journey, perhaps not unlike that of the readers, who, to some extent, may feel themselves drawn into aspects of the interplays highlighted in this poetic opus, a sentimental and questing echo...

Fernando M. Soares Silva

THE DANCE OF THE SEASONS

Mother Nature, please tell me:

Can the budding and flowery Spring
ever dance with the cold, somber Winter?
Can the early, sunny and warm Summer
ever kiss the defoliating Autumn?

Listen to me, oh you, inquiring heart:

The Seasons gyrate with each other,
embraced, in a never-ending dance,
ever hand-in-hand, and heart to heart,
as the world is propelled in the skies,
perpetually turning around and around
in the infinite vastness of the Universe...

The Sun of hot and relaxing Summers
and gentle, dreamy and romantic Springs,
is the same, the very same, that, tenderly,
osculates the falling leaves of Autumn
and gladdens the cold hearts of gelid Winter
with its Sunshine, bearer of good tidings...

How different is the cool morning dew
of the energetic mornings of Spring,
and of the lazy dawns of Summer season,
from the heavy and often castigating rain
falling down from above, the high heavens?
Both are an ardent kiss of love from me…

The furious, inclement and uncontrollable winds
---that, in Winter, Autumn and in other seasons,
seem to tear apart the innermost peace and quiet
of humans and other creatures in this vast world, ---
even they turn to mild, suave, and comforting breezes
to refresh and reinvigorate tired bodies and souls…

Even though distinct, one from another,
every one of the Seasons is interrelated
as each and all notes of a great symphony,
as the uninterrupted march of Nature
in Dawn, Day, Evening and Night,
just as a heart in love and love in a heart
evolve into a dance of ethereal beauty…

Come, sweetheart, dance as all Seasons do…
One Nature, One Heart, One Soul…
Let the rose petals of Spring and Summer
pirouette forever with Autumn and Winter
as they carpet and grace the many pathways,
perhaps short, perhaps long, but never impossible
of that dream of Happiness longing in your heart…"

4 – FERNAND M.S. SILVA

OTIOSE MOMENTS

Divagating morosely,
abstractly...
like spirals of smoke
ethereal,
in soporific curves,
my soul seeks Nirvana,
the indefinable peace!...

Who, What, Where are you?
In the depths of my heart?
No! Not in the dissatisfaction,
never in the confusion
and, alas, much less in the inquietude
which consumes me
 in utterly consumptive ashes! ...

Yet, I sense and I touch you,
vividly! ...
Your inexorable fascination,
indelible,
envelops my whole being
in an ineffable,
unavoidable embrace!

But, torment of torments,
Who, What, Where are you?
Perchance are you,
pray tell me,
are you that elusive vision
which escapes me?
Are you Happiness, Nirvana?

EMBRACING OBSESSION...

Enveloped in a long,
radiant, yet nebulous,
thin, diaphanous veil,
you hound me, incredulous,
a mere, pitiful wail
of an unfinished song...

Evade you I cannot, alas,
ubiquitous vision,
nightmare indelible,
cruel, yet sweet obsession,
symphony ineffable
of a phantasmal palace...

I hide in the dark meadows,
questing oblivion...
yet afraid of getting lost,
disappearing in confusion,
in the embracing innermost
of your eternal shadows...

Kiss me, obsession, tenderly,
in a hot fury, burning,
oh inescapable dream...
I come to you, again, searching,
for the refreshing stream
of my Destiny, eagerly...

HAUNTING SONG...

Everywhere I hear a song
vibrantly loud,
subtly, very faintly at times,
relentlessly
pursuing, enveloping me,
my whole being,
the innermost of heart and soul...

Here and there, that chant haunts me,
inexorably,
incessantly, pitilessly,
day and night, too,
in deep valleys or high mountains,
in midst of crowds
or the abysses of silence...

I stop, I pause, I walk, I run,
ever trying,
endeavoring to decipher,
perhaps evade
the mysterious, tenacious grasp
of that haunting
increasingly my soul hugging...

"What is it? "Who are you?", I ask,
wandering, puzzled...

"Are you the voice of Destiny,
maybe of Fate,
or the breath of the Being Supreme
persistently
whelming, overpowering me?"…

The song continues without pause,
ever present,
ubiquitous, omnipotent,
diaphanous,
enigmatic and obvious,
transfixing,
leaving me confused, exhausted…

In my complex perplexity
I cry, silent,
"Whatever, whoever you are,
ephemeral,
or perennial, it matters not,
love, oh! love me,
embrace me tenderly, tightly"…

"Let me repose my tired head
over your chest,
and in the deepest of your heart,
for evermore
enchanted by symphonies of love,
everlasting,
into endless eternity"…

HAPPINESS...

A sliver of a raindrop,
kissing the thirsty lips
of a lonely rose...
in the somber valley
just behind the faceless,
indifferent,
high mountain...

A hand extending a heart
to another human in need,
in the midst of sorrow...
buffeted by waves
of solitary despair,
cruelly,
miserably forgotten...

A smile in the cold night,
in the lost, confused shadows
of a tormented soul,
tossed by furious winds
of humanity's oblivion,
and hopeless,
shattered dreams...

A friendly, loving embrace
between two hearts, lost perhaps
in the paths of life...
struggling to grasp tightly
what is left to hope,
yet,
in the sea of existence...

SPIRALING DREAMS

Once upon a sweet time ago,
when the sun was bright and warm,
looking over verdant valleys
and unconquerable mountains
facing arrogant blue oceans,
I used to have soaring dreams…

Buffeted by ambitious winds,
my then naïve but intrepid mind
would spiral, unconcernedly,
up, up and up, always upwards
like the smoke of the big, gray ship
that later carried me away
to the wonders of the old Rome…

There were tears in my eyes
and intense, indescribable,
wrenching pain in my aching heart
as I said and waved goodbyes
to dear ones, some of whom,
alas, I would never see again…

But those golden, spiraling dreams,
ever dancing, pirouetting
in my avid and thirsty soul,
beckoned and enticed me
onwards, not unlike the legendary
sea mermaids of old sailors
who tamed the fustigating oceans…

What would be my destiny?
Only the Heavens above knew it,
as I indomitably surged,
puffed, ever pulled and pushed forward
just like a fabled ancient knight
rescuing his enchanting princess…

Still in search of new horizons
and questing wider frontiers
for my effervescent mind and heart,
I later flew, crossed many skies,
lands, continents and oceans
seemingly without end or borders…

As I on occasion glance back,
very often with deep nostalgia,
I still see, not yet dissipated,
those thin spirals of golden dreams
that, throughout life, have taught me
that one is never too old to dream…

BLUE SKIES

In the blue of the skies
I read unique pulchritude,
bliss, serenity anew…
And my heart bursts in sighs,
as I dream in solitude,
aching, questing for you…

All around me is peaceful,
very still and silent,
I am alone, yet I hear a pounding,
in my soul, powerful…
and feel unmistaken and ardent,
the touch of lips resounding…

Ineffable warmth seizes me,
my being enveloping…
Then, by my side, a voice I hear:
"For me and for thee,
there is still a rhapsody playing,
a love song not just to hear…"

I turned to the voice, whispering:
"Let's dance, my Sweetheart,
just you, darling, and I,
let's sing a song unending,
with the music of the heart…
Let's dance and pirouette
as high as the sky…"

STARING AT THE SEA...

There she was staring at the sea,
silently, serenely,
mesmerized by the bright sunshine
tenderly, amorously
osculating the vast, blue waters
fleetingly, teasingly
running towards the bay's beaches...

Who was she, to ask I dared not...
Perhaps a goddess,
wondering timidly I thought...
Perhaps in love,
reminiscing past, or present
heart throbbing Neptunes
or frolicking, tempting mermaids? ...

Staring at the sea, I could not tell...
But, oh, so suddenly,
in her eyes, I saw a tear drop
subtly, hesitantly,
as if absconding a story,
perhaps an epic,
or was it a dark nightmare?...

No! I did not dare to ask...
I already knew,
that the vast waters of the seas
of all the oceans
are the tears from the above,
gods and goddesses,
and humanity's love odysseys...

LONGING FOR YOU

Oh, how I long for you,
my darling,
in the midst of the night,
in the deafening silence
of my long vigil...

Tic-tac, tic-tac, tic-tac,
sings the clock,
my only visible companion
in the crushing solitude
of my dark cogitations...

Oh, how 1 long for you,
sweet honey,
as the shadows of emptiness,
merciless nightmare,
invade my wandering heart...

I dream of walking with you,
hand in hand,
through the verdant valleys
of joy and happiness,
our Promised Land...

Oh, how I long for you,
my love,
as I walk alone in the rain...
in the frigid and fustigating wind
of existence's storms...

Come... Come to me, sweet dream...
Embrace me tightly...
Let's find refuge and solace
in each other's caressing arms
and longing hearts...

Let me kiss you "good night",
gently, tenderly...
Let me whisper "my love" into your ears...
sweetly, adoringly...
Come... Hasten to me! ...

IN THE MIDDLE OF THE NIGHT

As the creeping night advances,
slowly, very slowly,
and darkness grows and grows denser,
heavier and thicker,
spectral shadows begin to soar,
whizzing and swishing
across the huge space in my mind,
shaken and buffeted
by myriad thoughts and images…

I toss and again turn over
my tired body
gasping for interval, a pause,
the illusive sleep,
groping hesitantly fumbling
floating ideas,
in vertiginous interplay
with my heart and soul
in gyrations mysterious…
Illusions clash with delusions,

hopes with fallen dreams,
blue skies with thunderous tempests
lightning with rainbows,
yesterdays with vague tomorrows,
rose petals with thorns,
all frenetically colliding
in a nightmare
of ghosts tormenting my sleep…

Illusions clash with delusions,
hopes with fallen dreams,
blue skies with thunderous tempests
lightning with rainbows,
yesterdays with vague tomorrows,
rose petals with thorns,
all frenetically colliding
in a nightmare
of ghosts tormenting my sleep…

Then, in midst of this hellish dance
a lucent vision,
brighter than even all sunshine,
suddenly appears,
the specters vanishing far away…
And osculating me
she whispers softly: Rest my Sweet!
Put your head on my chest,
and listen to my heart's music…
I am the peace, the Love you seek…

ALONE

Oh, how I feel lonely,
confused,
wandering aimlessly,
alone,
lost in the midst of roars
of crowds
of so different voices…

Oh, how I feel forlorn,
drifting,
roaming over high peaks,
green meadows
parched deserts, thorny bushes,
tossed
like a fallen, lifeless leaf…

Here and there, I stagger,
I stumble
groping phantasms, dead petals,
mere fragments
of visions yet unfulfilled,
chimeras,
perhaps, of my own self…

All seems dreary, meaningless,
so empty,
as I look around, everywhere,
in quest of
that ever-enchanting spring
that fulfills
my whole soul and thirsty heart...

Distant, very far away,
fleetingly,
I see tiny sparks, flashes,
glimpses,
of lights to me not unknown,
flickering,
as if beckoning me...

Away I turn my tired head,
eyes and heart,
 from illusions turned delusions,
 bouquets
 of wondrous flowers, and roses
 turned thorns...,
 as I, sad, whisper to myself
 I would rather be alone..."

DREAMING IN THE RAIN...

Softly, with a feathery touch,
tiny and lucent raindrops fall
on my cold, furrowed forehead,
as I ambulate pensively
labyrinths of my inner self
wandering, searching, questing...

I walk solitary, in silence,
seemingly a somnambulist,
in long, profound cogitations,
hearing just the soliloquy
of my groping and aching soul
hand in hand with my dreaming heart...

Raindrops keep falling tenderly,
caressing, soothing and kissing
my bruised, yet restless, thirsty lips
longing for the fusion of hearts
that quenches even the deserts
parched by the most inclement suns...

Then, I look up to skies above,
and what wondrous thing do I see?
Rainbows harbingers of sunshine,
renewed hope, faith, joy and laughter,
fulfillment of dreams yet to come
as I enshrine YOU in my heart...

DO YOU LOVE ME?

Do you love me? You ask me,
perhaps in trepidation
when troubled by somber skies
or the sound of far thunders
and fears of blinding lightning…

Honey, look into my eyes!
Can't you see, deep in my heart,
the high, ever blazing flames
burning, burning day and night,
overtaking my whole being?

Can't you hear the music
of those delightful moments
when I whisper most sweetly
into your avid ears
"Sunshine, Sweetheart, I love You"?

Don't you feel the heat, the warmth
with which I hold in my arms
your body, your heart and soul,
in my vehement, torrid
and unending embraces?

And when I caress you, softly,
as smoothly as a cool breeze
in blistering summer days,
don't you sense the ineffable,
wondrous touch of a heart in love?

Why, really, do I love you?
Is it destiny or fate?
No, mere chance it is not…
Just let me tell you, again,
I love you for you are YOU
and you, my Dear, love ME…

LOVE IS...

Love is...
when you open your soul's windows,
your eyes,
and, as a bird pirouetting in the blue sky,
a flashing star,
a splendorous spark of your heart
flies out dancing
and warmly touches me...

Love is...
when you softly, tenderly, caress me,
dreamily,
with your soft, velvety fingers...
reverberating
the melodious, polyphonic emotions
overflowing
from the innermost of your being...

Love is...
when you longingly, eagerly kiss me,
in a delirium,
in an outburst of true, burning desire
all-consuming,
a feverish passion that envelops you
and me
in a long rapture of ecstasy...

Love is...
when you and I, two beings, two lovers
in one heart...
seek shelter, and warmth in the glow
of our love,
in a fusion of two caring hearts and souls
made one,
for ever in an unending, flaming embrace...

HEARTBEAT OF LOVE

Exhausted, I enter my cocoon,
my soul's shelter,
refuge,
seeking peace, serenity,
a nirvana,
absorption, without extinction,
of my being…

Looking around, I see a light,
glowing warmly,
steadily,
over and over beckoning me,
enticingly,
to approach and recline
my tired head…

Hesitantly, in my confusion,
I stammer and murmur timidly
"Where?",
and the light soothingly whispers:
"Here,
in the safe harbor of my heart,
in my embrace"…

Incredulous, but, firmly, I reply:
"I have known the glow, the heat,
the inferno
of other seductive bright lights,
delusions,
dark nights of my existence…
"Who are you?"…

Smiling as no one ever before,
and enveloping tightly her heart
around mine,
she says, caressing softly my ears,
"I am LOVE,
the love you have been questing
in your dreams"…

Slowly, but, oh, so ever longingly,
I rested my head on her chest,
and, dreamily,
I heard her strong heartbeat
chanting,
singing to me new, enchanting
songs of love...

BOUQUET OF TRUE LOVE

As a refreshing summer breeze
at the end of a long, blistering day
seems to revive languid bodies,
and limp, deeply apathetic souls
grasping breathlessly for cool air,
you came so softly into my life…

You brought me new, radiant smiles,
promises of blue, vaster, wider skies,
and horizons of golden dreams
to be fulfilled in the longed heaven
of two hearts so deeply engulfed
in a spellbound, true embrace of love…

Away from your fascinating eyes
that deeply penetrate my heart
and spark lively, igniting flames
whose ardor seems to melt my soul,
I feel overwhelming emptiness
that tears the innermost of my being…

I miss your mellifluous touch
either in the brightness of the day
or amidst dark shadows of the night,
when deafening cries of loneliness
resonate deeply in my wandering soul,
marvelously entranced by you…

True love is ineffable, I know,
and words, even the most beautiful,
cannot ever fully depict
the authentic depth of our love,
just as the heights of the heavens
transcend all humanity's reason…

But I am singing, just chanting
as many, countless others have done
throughout each and all centuries,
in multiform poetic melodies,
the pulchritude of the grand bouquet
of a tender heart and unique soul…

I embrace you with passionate love,
for heartfelt "amor" from the profound
and innermost of your total self
is what you really are giving me…
Let's now smile, walk, your hand in my hand,
always with poetry in our hearts…

LOOKING INTO YOUR EYES

Caressing your velvety,
radiant face,
so tenderly
with ever dancing fingers,
tentacles of my soaring heart
swiveling high,
so far above mundane worries,
I always look into your eyes...

I stare fixedly at them,
the fascinating,
so glistening
wide windows of your soul,
and the sunny path to your heart
palpitating hard
as our anxious and thirsty lips touch
and fuse in a torrid embrace...

In your eyes I can see
unmistakably,
so vividly,
the immensity of the emotions
of your ever glowing love,
as we dance
cheek to cheek, heart to heart,
all day and all nightlong…

As I look into your eyes
gleaming stars,
far and near,
explode splendorous, varicolored,
one and all in the broad sky,
floating then
ever so gently down to earth
as we whisper to each other
"I love you"…

FOR EVER EMBRACING YOU

Out there, it's cruelly gelid,
very frigid, in the cold wilderness
of a world, oh! so indifferent,
and strangely insensitive
to humanity's most profound,
compelling instinct, force and need,
the fusion of minds, souls and hearts
into an embrace of real love…

Out there, it's cruelly gelid…
Broken hearts in bitter tears
mostly in maddening silence,
in solitary agony
even in midst of roaring crowds,
as the days evolve into nights
and dark nights into nightmares,
plunging one's self into emptiness…

Out there, it's cruelly gelid...
I hear your sobs and see your tears
rolling down, like shining diamonds,
stubbornly dripping from your eyes
so loving, trusting and giving,
but still deeply wondering
whether true shelter and solace
can ever be found for your heart...

Out there, it's cruelly gelid...
But, let it go!... Look into my eyes...
What matters the cold of winter
and the falling leaves of autumn
if there is a flowering spring
and a sunny summer just ahead
as I whisper into your ears:
I am forever embracing you!

SYMPHONY OF LOVE...

What does time matter to us
enraptured, immersed in love,
oblivious of a cold world
and its dissonant noises,
if listening to our hearts
we hear the most beautiful,
enchanting symphony of love?

Gazing into your sweet eyes,
I see the depths of your soul,
the roaring waves of emotion
overflowing your total being,
now, like a golden poppy,
stretching its longing petals,
to the kisses of sunshine…

Gently touching your dear face
I feel your inner vibrations,
and I sense your intensity,
vivid, clear, ineffable,
as the sounds of a guitar
playing deep, romantic tunes
In the middle of the night...

Caressing you tenderly,
as you, in a deep trance, dream...
I perceive your palpitations,
the heartbeats of your passion,
and, embracing you ardently,
I drop, falling at your knees,
singing a symphony of love...

UNFINISHED RHAPSODY

Come near, very close, my darling,
rest your palpitating heart
on my lonely chest…
And hear my soul's sighs
as I tell you a story,
indeed a secret…
bits, great chunks of me,
amidst the haunting sounds
of an unfinished rhapsody…

As you look deeply into my eyes,
what do you see?
Perhaps the boldness of a winner
who defied lofty waves
as he subjugated furious Neptunes? …
Or do you still perceive
remnants of bitter tears
along with pestering disquiet,
deep, deep in my heart?

Yes, sweetheart, haunting fears
still trouble and shake my heart...
Fears not of you, darling, my sweet,
but trepidations of distracting you
in your quest for real happiness
and dreams everlasting...
Spring and Winter don't dance together
nor does the Morning Sun kiss Sunset
the harbinger of time's end...

Yet, I feel impelled, drawn
to embrace you, oh! so tightly,
and to love you ardently,
as the ever haunting sounds
of an ineffably beautiful music
overwhelm my whole being,
body, mind, heart and soul,
in a quasi Nirvana stupor
by poets called "amor"...

Come very close to me, sweetheart,
come and hear the melodies of love,
a new love vibrant, yet so tender,
perhaps made in the Olympus
where singing angels and butterflies
pirouette, floating high in space,
oblivious of the boundaries of time,
and the world's many sorrows,
in a never ending dream...

COME, COME TO ME! ...

As the nigh approaches
tenebrous,
shadowing all nature,
humans, too,
with a cloak of mystery...
I, pensive,
think of you, my darling,
only you,
as I listen to my heart...

Ardent, I toss and turn
groping for you
as I rest my fiery head
on the bed
of the huge volcano,
my imagination,
where I see you, sweetheart,
and softly say
"Dearest! Come, come to me"...

Morpheus I don't need
to have dreams
and sing gloriously
in my heart,
in the middle of the night,
as I see you,
beautiful, soundly asleep,
by my side,
as I whisper " I love you!"…

Looking at you, my Sunshine,
I see stars,
myriads of bright galaxies,
winkingly
smiling at each other
as we dream,
kiss, caress, embrace
and love, saying,
"Sweetheart! Come, come to me"…

TWO HEARTS, ONE SOUL...

Why have our existential paths
crossed and merged? ...
Why have the seasons of our lives,
Summer and Winter,
embraced, twirled and danced cheek to cheek,
in unique rapture,
in fiery, overwhelming emotions?

Is it true love what so strongly binds us
to one another?
You hear my heart loudly pounding,
when you rest your head
on my aching and vibrating chest...
I hear the symphony of your soul,
just looking at you...

But, dear Sweetheart, what's being in love?
Just ethereal bliss
of bodies burning in hot passion,
mindless of a world
gelid, often barbarous, savage? ...
Or is it an embrace of two hearts
fusing in one soul?

Let's kiss again, once more and again,
a thousand times,
and again as we cling to each other
wholly, heart to heart,
lips to lips, soul-to-soul, whispering
"I love you, Sweetheart"
for ever, and ever more, throughout time…

Let's merge our hearts and souls!

LOVEBIRDS

Swiveling, swiveling high
in the blue sky,
humming and humming
ever happy,
two beautiful birds
necking and necking
dance and chant and sing
symphonies of love
never before
by human hearts heard…

Flipping, flipping high
over mountains
peaks and deep valleys,
they float and turn,
zooming all over,
mindless, oblivious
but of themselves,
two birds, two hearts,
fused in one embrace,
in loving dreams…

Flying over rainbows
their wings they spread,
then hugging each other,
oh, so tightly,
they hover softly
'round the flowers,
roses, carnations,
kissing, then drinking
the morning dew
dripping from their hearts...

And as they whisper
sweetly, dreamily,
"Darling, I Love You",
poems of true love,
the world smiles,
nature rejoices,
and sunshine returns
to warm all hearts,
all corners of Earth
with a kiss of love...

THE MUSIC THAT WE MAKE

In the hypnotic undulation
of your longing heart,
when lively waves of nostalgia
rock and roll your yearning soul,
you whisper, at times,
softly, as only you can do,
"Write me a new poem, Sweetheart"…

Upon hearing your questing words,
as if Neptune I were,
I command the winds to subside
and the waves to frolic away
so none would disturb us
as we compose unique verses
only by us fully understood…

I embrace you, you embrace me…
We offer kisses,
hundreds, thousands, why not millions?
in a symphony of caresses,
as we grope ardently
for each other, each other's hearts,
hearing the music that we make…

Love poems cannot be singly
conceived or composed,
for the true poetry of the heart
needs to be sung, danced and lived,
always and ever more,
in a fusion of body and soul,
in unending chorus of joy...

IN THE MOONLIGHT

On a calm, bright, and refreshing night,
as we walked hand in hand
under the hypnotic gaze above,
distant, very far away,
of the high, seemingly smiling moon,
I heard her whispering to me
"What's the moon, and why does it smile?
Please, oh please, my darling, do tell me"…

I looked at her, at her shining eyes,
and tried to decipher
whether those flickering, brilliant glints
were wandering thoughts, lustrous gems,
the reflection of her noble soul,
perhaps her heart, or both,
flashing in the caressing moonlight
as a welcoming beacon of love…

Somewhat perplexed and groping for words,
I looked upwards at the moon,
and, then, into her expecting eyes…
I embraced her tenderly
as we sat under a leafy tree
by the side of a pond
mirroring the moon high above
and the beauties of the tree and her…

It was a night serene, mysterious,
when the universe hugs you
and the world seems so harmonious,
as if in a kissing mood…
So, I osculated her more than once,
as many times as the stars
floating, dancing, laughing in the skies,
looking upon us both with special joy…

Still marveling at the great beauty
that enveloped her and me,
I gently pulled her towards my chest
and, with heart palpitating,
I said: "Darling, rest your head on me,
while I tell you a secret…
I will now tell you about that moon
that shines so enigmatically…"

Trustingly, she reclined close to me,
her heart racing furiously
and mine resounding in unison…
Whispering, I commenced:
"The moon is the hiding place
of love secrets of humanity…
The lighted side that we see
is the one ardently kissed by the sun…"

"The other, the supposedly dark face,
mysterious always,
is where the key to Man's love secrets,
odysseys, and our destinies
is kept, absconded, guarded
by whom or what, we will never know…
Oh! I wish I had that key
 to decipher Destiny, yours and mine…"

"The other, the supposedly dark face,
mysterious always,
is where the key to Man's love secrets,
odysseys, and our destinies
is kept, absconded, guarded
by whom or what, we will never know…
Oh! I wish I had that key
to decipher Destiny, yours and mine…"

Hearing all these words, she grabbed my head,
looked deeply into my eyes,
and said: "I see your entire soul
and the labyrinths to your heart,
the key to destiny, yours and mine…
As you pierce into my being
can you really feel and say the same,
that our destiny is one?"…

In response, I pulled her ever closer
in an ending embrace,
in a fusion of hearts and souls…
Around us, Nature was still,
as if listening to our sweet whispers,
while the moonlight above
gradually faded away…
ushering in a new bright dawn and day…

WHISPERING I LOVE YOU...

Come to me, my darling sweetheart,
close, always closer...
Let's hear the palpitations
of both our hearts,
and the vibrations of the soul,
yours and also mine,
as we two sing, in unison,
sweet melodies,
"Fados" of enchanting love...

Let beautiful music resound
here, everywhere...
Let's make our incessant hands
and charged fingers
the strings of our golden guitars
magically stroking
and punctuating all the chords
of the heart and soul
in an unending ecstasy...

Let's kiss each other so smoothly
as a fine wine,
yet so ardently as the fire
and all the passion
that burn and consume our beings…
Let's, deep in rapture,
embrace one another in bliss,
elated, mindless
of a cruel and insane world…

Let's twirl, jump high and pirouette
in our love dance…
And savoring Venus' nectar,
lifted to high skies,
let's embrace even more tightly…
And, still caressing,
fusing hearts in endless kisses,
let's fall asleep in each other's arms
whispering "I Love You"…

I WISH I WERE A LITTLE BIRD

Oh, I wish I were a little bird,
perhaps a swallow,
so I could pirouette in the sky,
sing, dance in the air,
fly to places near and far, too,
over the mountains,
verdant valleys with trees and flowers,
wherever there is peace,
and love, if I could take you with me…

We would fly together, wing in wing,
cheek to cheek, laughing,
humming and purring sweet songs of joy,
again and again,
as we swooped down over the rivers,
placid lakes, oceans,
meadows, forests, even dry deserts,
wherever there is peace,
and love, harmony, tranquility…

Soaring over the entire Earth,
we would find a nest,
as soft as amorous hearts can be,
just for you and me,
replete with fervent hopes, golden dreams,
roses without thorns,
so you and I could rest our heads,
and, in unison,
intone most enchanting melodies…

In the incipient hours of dawn,
when sunshine first smiles,
opening my eyes and seeing you asleep,
I would wake you up
with a soft, gentle, yet ardent kiss,
and whisper tenderly:
"Honey, a new day has arisen;
Let's fly and hum again
a new song of love and harmony"…

OPEN YOUR HEART

Walking, hesitantly, as a somnambulant,
in the middle of a dark night,
you grope diaphanous, ethereal phantasms,
flashes of a gnawing despondency
in your tormenting quest for love...

In the deafening silence of your agony,
you trip, waver and fall,
sporadically pursuing tremulous specters,
fleeting lights at the end of the tunnel
of your tortured heart and soul...

In your confusion, you are totally oblivious,
unmindful of the ubiquitous,
cruel loneliness pervading the hearts
of your fellow beings in sorrow,
broken, wretched bits of humanity...

Listen! Don't you hear bitter, sad crying?
Those tears come from your soul,
bewildered, scared and utterly shredded
by your selfish loneliness,
by the uncertainty that consumes you…

Halt! Wake up... Open your tired eyes,
and stretching your empty arms,
embrace the loving flutter that passes you by
quivering, absconded, perhaps,
like you, in deforming anonymity...

Open your arms and your troubled soul,
as a flower greets the morning sun,
the warmth of its tender, invigorating kisses,
after a long, tempestuous night...
The sun has risen… Open your heart! ...

DO YOU REMEMBER?

Do you remember those words
whispered sweetly and often,
in the midst of our torrid moments
of a passion that seemed ever radiant,
all-defiant, enormous, uncontrollable,
oblivious of the turbulent world
that roared, unknowingly, about us?

Do you remember those embraces
that caressed you in my avid arms,
and chained your chest tightly to my heart
pulsating furiously, yet sweetly,
as we played wondrous rhapsodies
of a love that seemed so fulfilling,
so quenching the thirst that consumed us?

Do you remember those ardent kisses
that I poured over your glowing face
as we looked serenely at each other's eyes,
as I stroked you with never stopping fingers,
reflecting the Vesuvian emotions of my soul,
the profound depth of my feelings for you,
for what, to me, was the ultimate love?

I believed it when you said you loved me,
and in return I gave you my whole heart,
with all its dimensions and the intensity
that vibrated from a soul all-trusting,
allowing no other distractions or detours,
just happy to have you enshrined in my mind
as my queen, the treasure of my being…

Do you still remember those sweet hours,
unforgettable moments of ineffable happiness,
as we now stare at far, far away horizons,
no longer together, but driven apart
by somber skies and the distances in our souls,
and by those gelid winds that, ever increasingly,
have blown away golden dreams, and sweet memories?

LET ME HOLD YOU,
IMPOSSIBLE DREAM!

We must say goodbye,
farewell...
Torn hearts, shattered illusions,
our love, our burning passion
just another
impossible dream...

But wait, my Love! …

Let me hold you to my heart,
tightly...
Let me fix those radiant jewels,
your tender and loving eyes,
in the emptiness
of my broken soul...

Hold me, my Sweet!
Let me touch your silky hair,
once more, my Love...
Let my fingers caress you,
your dreamy face,
your gentle body,
passionately...

Kiss me... Kiss me! …

Let me kiss you, my Dream,
anew...
Let me forget my sorrow,
this Impossible Dream
of my inexorable destiny...
in your love...

Let me hold you!

GONE WITH THE WIND

Once upon a time,
far and also not so long ago,
oh! I had a dream,
so refulgent and so beautiful,
of unending love…

Quixotically,
and confusedly, I staggered
now here, now there,
seemingly all over the universe,
searching and questing…

Glory I ignored,
riches, fame, to me little mattered,
but just an embrace,
warm, tender, not ever deceitful,
where my head could rest…

Fearless, I braved
storms, hurricanes, thunders and lightning,
sent by Mother Nature
or by evil inhumanity,
often in the past…

I have conquered all…
But, like the fabled Don Quixote,
I felt cold, empty
as a freezing, cruel, gelid wind
blew away my dream…

Now, in my Sunset
peace and harmony I encounter,
perhaps contentment…
Is this the elusive, quested dream,
inexpugnable,
even by the strongest, frigid wind?

SOUL SEARCHING

Once upon a time, now very distant,
far, far away,
when I was naïve and so very young,
still with little golden curls flowing down
so freely and loosely,
over my serene and unwrinkled forehead...
when I would let my wild imagination
fly daringly high
and build great, huge, magnificent castles
in the resplendent dream factory
of my restless, so effervescent mind,
there was a question,
a most persistent interrogation
that as a shadowy ghost haunted me
as I sought to decipher "WHAT am I?"

As the years rolled by, some slowly,
some vertiginously,
and many dreams became fulfilled quests
ever so gleaming under the blue sky,
just like diamonds
shining on the haughty warrior's helmet
that I had thought then to be wearing,
so quixotically,
the old question turned philosophical
as I, matured, became introspective
and searched feverishly for the real meaning
of my own self,
of my being and essence in this world
where confusion and madness rein supreme...
and I began to ask: "WHO am I?"

Now, several and long decades later,
white and cold snow
has fallen on my humbler, wiser head,
whose forehead no longer unwrinkled
shows deep furrows,
the disquieting puzzling that haunts me
stirring my quivering mind, heart and soul
relentlessly,
as I wander through the narrow paths
of my own existential sunset
still wondering no longer about
WHAT am I, or WHO am I,
but murmuring, in bewilderment,

why, Heavens, oh why, please tell me,
why? why? "WHY am I?

SUNSET...

As sunset approaches
subtly,
slowly pushing away
the pallid, fading sun
far and farther
into distant horizons...
I let my heart wander,
feeling,
ever so vividly,
the enveloping darkness
in my body and soul...

Thoughts of now remote,
but once bright,
radiant hours and days,
moments of unforgettable joy,
hurrahs and glory,
still flicker in my mind...
as the advancing shadows
persistently
hug and squeeze me,
without mercy,
ever more tightly...

Where are now those roses,
oh, so beautiful,
that charmed the pathways
of my existential odyssey,
once upon a time
when I was still young,
and not so young,
when I smelled the perfumed
enchanting petals,
oblivious of the thorns
that would tear my heart? ...

Oh, let it go! Let it go! ...
In the growing darkness
I still glimpse,
so clearly,
the torrents of hot sweat
and the tears, too,
with which I dared to imagine
and realize epic dreams,
while fighting huge monsters,
multiform and horrendous,
on the way through Calvary...

Looking around, I pause…
and breathlessly
I listen to the shadows
now whispering,
pointing with thin, glacial fingers
to what seems a dawn,
yet another dawn…
and new, rosy horizons
tantalizing but terrifying
as my soul is drawn to them,
whirling uncontrollably, helplessly…

What is there? What else is there?
Puzzled, I ask myself
trying to decipher the unknown,
struggling to penetrate
the Infinite's iron curtains…
More lights? More laurels?
Perhaps more thorny roses?
Oh, let them go! …
Don Quixote I am not
and golden windmills are no longer…
Just illusory delusions…

Unfeelingly, the dark shadows
turn into night,
bidding goodbye to the sunset,
plunging me, oh, so solitary,
lonely…
into a quest for identity,
a dream of further fulfillment,
almost a nightmare…
as I, confused and exhausted,
whisper, soporifically,
"just let me sleep"…

ETERNAL TEARS...

My soul cries tears,
eternal,
for you, my darling,
my love…
now resting,
sleeping in peace,
in Eternity...

You went away,
so fast,
so silently,
in a vertigo of grief,
broken hearts,
and impossible,
unspoken goodbyes...

No longer can I,
my love,
embrace you with tenderness...
or touch your hair,
those loving hands...
or feel the warmth
of your eyes...

I cry lonely,
in immense,
anguished grief...
for you, eternally...
light of my soul,
love of my heart,
forever! ...

ONCE UPON A TIME

Once upon a time,
yet not long ago,
my heart let me know it
and my eyes could see,
there was music,
enchanting poesy
in sapphire skies,
in verdant valleys,
in blue and gray seas
and in the deep oceans,
on hills and mountains,
in flowers and trees,
in the whole nature…

76 – FERNAND M.S. SILVA

Once upon a time,
yet not far away,
when I looked at the world
of enormous mass
of humanity,
I could see and feel in it
not just bodies, but hearts,
not just faces, but souls
full of hopes and dreams,
sighs, aspirations,
ardently questing
pathways to happiness,
real bliss...

Once upon a time,
I had a golden dream...
Perhaps I was naive,
but I wished, oh I wished,
all tears and heartbreaks,
illness and disease,
sorrows, bitterness,
hunger add thirst,
hatred and violence
to disappear,
forever vanish
from the face of Earth,
from all human hearts...

Once upon a time,
near and long ago,
there was poetry
in hearts and souls…
There were poems,
song and rhapsody,
dancing, symphony,
in and around the world,
fleetingly, although …
There was music and hope, too,
in the hearts and minds
of fellow human beings
in all corners of the earth…

Once upon a time,
there was poetry,
oh, indeed, there was…
Why does it seem to have vanished
from the air and the horizons?
Mornings are somber,
sunsets are darker,
sunshine is colder,
and so, too, is life…
Wondering aloud,
now I ask myself:
Is poetry, the echo of the soul,
mere fiction of dreaming,
aching hearts?

I CRY IN THE WIND...

I cry …lonely,
in the midst of roaring crowds
deaf,
indifferent to my agony...

"Who am I?"
I shout, wandering...
illusive specter
of a pallid,
moribund candlelight...

God! My God!
Who am I?
Ruins of golden castles,
mere windblown feather,
tossed
in the oblivion of eternity...

Let me cry! …

Broken dreams,
empty laughter,
foolish loves,
desperate,
tearless tears...

I cry in the wind,
in the tempests of existence
my destiny,
my sorrow,
my nothingness! ...

Let me cry... in the wind!

DON'T SEND ME FLOWERS...

When I pass away
to regions unknown,
far, far away…
don't send me flowers,
not even a rose,
or a fallen leaf...

Don't kill a flower
or harm a petal,
anywhere...
to remember my passing
on this earth,
also theirs...

Don't send me flowers,
but just a tear,
warm and sincere...
if we meant something
to each other...
if you still love me...

And if you do,
keep me in your heart,
and in your dreams...
Thus, we will never die,
you and I,
forever...

SCINTILLATING LIGHTS

Once upon a long, long time ago
when I was a little, tiny child
and the world did not appear cold,
nor violent, cruel or insane,
I used to look at those distant stars
up there, far, in the high skies above
like a phantasmagoric mantle...

Soon, I would fall into a trance,
as if magical incantation,
perhaps a heavenly lullaby,
had carried me, ever so gently,
to far away lands of mystery
where fantasy and reality
merge into drams of pure delight...

I was then a little, tiny child,
but, oh my Lord, I could, indeed, dream
of silver fairies, golden castles
and lots and lots of friendship and love
everywhere, in all corners of Earth
where humans exist, live and also toil
often mindless of one another...

Still dreaming of those luminous stars
twinkling brightly in the dark of night,
I used to gaze, in fascination,
at the simple, often crude mangers
where older siblings, and I also,
had placed the baby Jesus asleep,
floating angels softly singing around...

Little wax candles adorned the scene,
flickering at the slightest motion
as if laughing and dancing in joy,
basking in Christmas festivities,
happy to warm the little baby,
as our tender hearts vibrated
to sounds of unforgotten carols...

As changing times and ways often do
multicolored lights, in all sizes,
soon pushed away the little candles
and their nuances of mystery...
Yet, even polychromatic lights
have a mellifluous charm of their own
as they kindle and caress the hearts...

Now, no longer a little sweet child,
as I wander pensive in Sunset's dusk
I ask myself: Where, where did time go?
All I know is that it has flown by,
vanished so fast, vertiginously,
seemingly as daylight turns to night,
and summer jumps into freezing winter...

I am no longer a tiny child,
but, oh my Lord, I can and still dream...
As I gaze at those far away stars
and at the bright, scintillating lights
on trees by little Jesus' manger,
I dream of God's blessings, peace and love,
Christmas' true calling and meaning...

Twinkling, twinkling distant little stars
shine brightly to us day and night...
Dance, pirouette with all Christmas lights,
red, blue, white and the other colors...
Warm up our hearts with thoughts of love,
serenity and true peace of mind
in a tight, everlasting embrace...

DOMINAE PULCHRAE...

Quondam, me esse equitem somniavi
orbem terrarum percurrentem,
arma fulgentia in manibus portantem
omnes et omnia lacessentem,
ubique et semper felicitatem quaerentem
in maribus, in montibus, in vallibus,
in urbibus, in foris hominum, ubique...

Frustra, totum mundum percucurri
nihil aliud nisi frustrationem inveniens,
nisi aliud praeter inanitatem acerbam,
tristitiam, delusionem et lacrimas.
Tristis, dolens, in magno dolore meo,
scrutationem meam tunc exii,
in aeternum, sic iuravi...

Dies, noctes, tempestates, et anni ierunt...
sed cor meum, vacuum, solum
et amoris, amoris urentis egens et avidum,
magnum, patens, et generosum remanebat...
Tunc, repente, felicitas in specie amoris vivificantis
leniter apparuit maximo cum fulgore,
et dulce nomen eius Nirvana erat...

TUNC SIDERA EFFERVERUNT...

Cum caeruleae revolventesque undae maris
in immensis arenis orae luderent ludibundae,
et subridentes furtive atque curiose spectarent
sub divo et sub sole latente, nebuloso,
illa et ille amantes incendentes, ardentes
in flammis mirabilibus dulcis amoris novi
aethera magnis clamonibus et subditis vagitibus
impleverunt, dum volucres omnium colorum,
parvi et ingentes, carmina laeta cantabant,
et sol cum luna maximo cum gaudio saltabant,
et in caelo toto fulgida sidera effervescebant...

86 – FERNAND M.S. SILVA

SUB NOCTEM...

"Et sub noctem, postquam domina discesserat,
caelum, triste atque "saudade" commotum,
lacrimas plurimas effudit, et, tunc,
illas rosas pulcherrimas a bella domina allatas,
et ab eo in horto suo cum diligentia sertas,
pluvia copiosissima cum amore basiavit ...""

Printed in the United States
40513LVS00005B/1-102

THE
ANCESTORS WITHIN

REVEAL AND HEAL THE ANCIENT MEMORIES YOU CARRY

AMY GILLESPIE DOUGHERTY

FEATURING: REV. ASHERAH ALLEN, ARIELLE, DR. ALLISON BROWN, DEENA CHESTER,
TANYA L. COLUCCI, CAROL DUTTON, M.J. GRAVES, ROBIN IVY HAYWOOD,
JONIANNE JEANNETTE, JACQUELINE M KANE, JAMES KEALIIPIILANI KAWAINUI,
ELIZABETH R KIPP, SONDRA LAMBERT, RIKA RIVKA MARKEL, LISA A. NEWTON, JEN PICENO,
DR. AHRIANA PLATTEN, CRYSTAL RASMUSSEN, MARCIA COLVER REICHERT, JEANNE RUCZHAK-ECKMAN,
NOAH SMITH, MYRNA Y. TRIANO, MICHELLE TROUPE, PHOENIX TRUEBLOOD